Gamal Abdel Nasser: The Life and Legacy of Egypt's Second President

By Charles River Editors

Nasser and Nikita Khrushchev

About Charles River Editors

Charles River Editors provides superior editing and original writing services to create digital content for publishers across a vast range of subject matter. In addition to providing original digital content for third party publishers, Charles River Editors republishes civilization's greatest literary works, bringing them to a new generation via ebooks.

Sign up here to receive updates about free books as we publish them, and visit Our Kindle Author Page to browse today's free promotions and our most recently published Kindle titles.

Introduction

Nasser (1918-1970)

"Our path to Palestine will not be covered with a red carpet or with yellow sand. Our path to Palestine will be covered with blood… In order that we may liberate Palestine, the Arab nation must unite, the Arab armies must unite, and a unified plan of action must be established." - Nasser

Gamal Abdel Nasser has been called many things. The father of modern-day Egypt. The founder of Arab nationalism. The leader of the Egyptian Revolution. The second president of the Egyptian Republic. The creator of his own brand of political and social governance – Nasserism. Anthony Eden, the former British Prime Minister, called him the "Mussolini of the Nile."

Nasser was all of these things and much more. Indeed, he led the revolution that overthrew the monarchy of Egypt and subsequently shaped and led the new Egyptian government. He became a prominent regional and world leader, playing a significant role in the Non-Alignment Movement that he co-founded, formed during the midst of the Cold War. He led his country toward modernization and industrialization, implementing social and economic reforms focused on strengthening the nation and improving the lives of the people. Yet, Nasser's legacy goes beyond state governance and policies; his name, to this day, evokes great emotion among Egyptians and much of the Arab world. His funeral in 1970 drew millions of mourners and an outpouring of genuine grief across the Arab world. Nasser continues to remain an iconic figure in the region, symbolizing Arab dignity, pride, and unity.

The country of Egypt has a turbulent past, and though today it is one of the most powerful regional powers in the Middle East, it had not been so for many centuries. The country lacked adequate natural resources with which to feed a hungry and growing population, and as with many Middle Eastern societies, suffered from a parasitic bureaucracy, in conjunction with colonialism and imperialism. Though the country boasted a glorious ancient past, once notable traditions and customs had long since faded away, giving way to a political, economic, and societal stagnation that was further nurtured by successive foreign occupations. Egypt was in decline.

Then came Gamal Abdel Nasser, son of a small village postal worker. Much of the most radical changes in mid-twentieth century Egypt – both progressive and not – can be traced to this one man, who was undeniably one of the strongest Middle East leaders of the last century. Born to a poor family with limited opportunities, Nasser rose through the ranks of the Egyptian military, developed a stellar insight for politics and military tactics, and eventually helped lead a revolution that overthrew the last Egyptian king, bringing about the end of the Egyptian monarchy. He then became president of the new nation, then leader of the entire Middle East region as he faced down the superpowers of the world and strove to keep Egypt independent from American and Soviet influence during the Cold War. He concentrated on making Egypt strong and proud again, his sole focus being the liberation of the Egyptian people from the chains of colonialism.

In addition to working to carve a path for a new Egypt, Nasser aimed to help the rest of the Arab nations of the Middle East by uniting the historically uncooperative Arab countries and encouraging them to act as a united front. Nasser was not the first to see that Arab countries more often than not had much in common, including resources, political policies, and social structures, but he was the first to take action and work to get the Arab countries to work together. The concept of pan-Arabism that Nasser furthered during his presidency had lasting impact on the region that continued decades after his death.

As such, Gamal Abdel Nasser made a significant mark on the regional and global politics of the 20th century. Though not many were his supporters, and fewer were his friend, all were aware of his influence and capabilities. Many of the other Arab leaders of the region feared him for his eloquence and his ability to inspire millions using only words, whether written or spoken; they were afraid he would incite their own populations to revolt. In other areas of the world, the British sought ways to reestablish their dominance over the Egyptian government, the Soviets worried that their friendship with Nasser had a deadline, and the Americans worried that Nasser would turn all of the Middle East against them. And the greatest anxiety over Egypt was held by the Israelis, who feared that Nasser was the one leader who could truly unite the Arab nations against them. But everyone, from his friends and supporters to his enemies, acknowledged and respected his bravery, idealism, and devotion to his country and people.

Gamal Abdel Nasser: The Life and Legacy of Egypt's Second President examines the life and legacy of one of the Middle East's most influential leaders, from his early life and military career to his role in the 1952 revolution. This book also explores his turbulent presidency and his lasting legacy. Along with a bibliography and pictures of important people, places, and events, you will learn about Nasser like never before, in no time at all.

Gamal Abdel Nasser: The Life and Legacy of Egypt's Second President

About Charles River Editors

Introduction

Chapter 1: Nasser's Early Years

Nasser as a teen in 1931

On January 15, 1918, Gamal Abdel Nasser was born in Beni Morr, a small village located near the city of Alexandria in Upper Egypt. He was the first son of Abdel-Nasser Hussein, a strong father and hard worker, who ran a small local post office in the village. Life in Beni Morr was difficult, as the town had little money, and Nasser's family even less. Much of the village population was either unemployed, or employed but still struggling to survive.[1] Nasser was thus raised in one of the many underdeveloped areas of Egypt, experiencing poverty and lack of basic services, which would gradually shape his mindset and vision for the future of his country. Furthermore, Nasser's biographers Robert Stephens and Said Aburish also wrote about the impact of Nasser's family on molding Nasser's views and ideas; they concluded that Nasser's family had been strong believers of Arab pride, nationalism, and the "Arab notion of glory," as one of Nasser's younger brothers was named Izz al-Arab, which directly translates to "glory of the Arabs" – a rare name in Egypt.[2]

Nasser was only two years old when he experienced his first brush with the chains of

---

[1] Sam Witte, *Gamal Abdel Nasser* (New York: Rosen, 2004), 9.
[2] Said K. Aburish, *Nasser: The Last Arab* (New York: St. Martin's Press, 2004), 13.

colonialism. In 1920, Nasser's uncle Khalil Hussein disappeared; it was only some time later that the family learned that he had been arrested for organizing and participating in anti-British demonstrations. Nasser's uncle was not the first, and he certainly would not be the last; anti-British sentiment was rampant as Egyptians called for complete self-governance and independence from Britain. Yet, Nasser's father was neither proud nor disapproving of his brother's actions; he was instead fearful, for he thought his brother's actions may cost him his job and possibly even his and his family's freedom. He decided then that his family would be completely removed from politics of any kind, and sought to teach Nasser to stay away from radical activities.[3]

The historical context in which Nasser was born and raised is vital to gaining an understanding of his beliefs and later actions. As with many leaders and seminal figures. In past and present geopolitical discussions, the Middle East is often reduced to "Israel and the Arab countries," as though these Arab nations are united by anything other than ethnic and religious tradition. This is largely inaccurate; each Arab nation is a distinct and separate country, consisting of its own unique history, economic principles, and government structure. Jordan had and still continues to have a strong monarchical system, whereas Lebanon developed a unique governance system of confessionalism, in which the three highest posts in the country are allocated along religious lines, to be held by a Maronite Christian, a Shi'a Muslim, and a Sunni Muslim. Among these varying countries, Egypt is perhaps one of the most distinct, as it has undergone such radical and far-reaching changes in the last century.

In 1900, Egypt was a monarchy, under the control of a hereditary king. All other power revolved around the elite noble class, which was unsurprisingly at the expense of the suffering lower peasant class. However, with the coming of the twentieth century, and following the pattern of other colonized nations calling for self-determination, a new nationalist movement was founded and developed in Egypt, born out of the frustrations and disappointments of the preceding century. Under the rallying cry of "Egypt for the Egyptians," these nationalists molded the widespread resentment and humiliation felt by the people into an embryonic political movement that began to grow in strength and numbers.[4]

Finally, after four decades as a British protectorate, Egypt gained independence from Britain in February 1922. However, this eventually proved to be a nominal freedom, as the country was still very much under the control of its former colonizer, and Britain continued to maintain a strong military presence in Egypt. In the areas that British powers receded, local autocrats claimed for themselves, capturing many sectors of the government and state administration. Though Egypt was renamed in its post-independence days as the Kingdom of Egypt, the country's sovereignty was nonetheless subject to severe restrictions imposed by the British; despite the fact that it had been declared free and independent, the kingdom continued to

---

[3] Witte, *Gamal Abdel Nasser*, 9.
[4] Keith Wheelock, *Nasser's New Egypt* (New York: Frederick A. Prager, Inc., 1960), 1.

experience significant British influence and intervention in its political, fiscal, administrative, and governmental affairs. Additionally, Britain retained its control of the Suez Canal – a key waterway for trade and transportation, and a primary interest of Britain and other European powers. The Egyptian people were disheartened and frustrated by this "independence," which was in truth just a continuation of the status quo under a different name. Furthermore, with powerful landowners firmly entrenched in the country's government, Egypt could scarcely expect to attain economic and social development, stunting its progress and modernization.

In the early 1920s, the nationalist Wafd party gained popularity, quickly becoming one of the most influential and active political parties in post-independence Egypt. Literally translating to "the delegation" in English, the Wafd party fervently opposed European interference in Egyptian affairs and called for the immediate termination of British occupation, thereby representing the voice and anger of many Egyptians tired of their country being utilized for the benefit of foreign powers, and at the expense of the domestic population. Uprisings, riots, and rallies were organized by the Wafd, and the party steadily grew to become Egypt's preeminent political party. In the 1924 parliamentary elections, the Wafd won an astonishing 179 of 211 parliamentary seats, firmly placing itself in the government, and in 1936, the Wafd again won 89% of the vote and 157 of 211 seats.[5]

It was in this nationalistic environment that Gamal Abdel Nasser was born and raised, during a time when the spirit of nationalism and anti-colonialism permeated throughout the country. Though his family shied away from the burgeoning fervor of the nationalist movement, Nasser would find himself in its midst.

When he was eight and ready to enter primary school, Nasser was sent by his father to Cairo for his education. By this time, his uncle Khalil, who had been arrested by the authorities for anti-government activities, was out of prison and living in Cairo; Nasser decided to stay with him. This was Nasser's first time out of his small and impoverished village, his first experience of city life. Living far away from his parents in an unfamiliar environment, young Nasser developed self-independence, but also leaned on his uncle for support, and Khalil in turn provided Nasser with lessons and stories of British imperialism. Nasser was radicalized by his uncle's stories, and he was also astonished by the filth and poverty that was rampant in Cairo, further strengthening his budding belief that something was wrong with the current state of his country. He eventually moved to Alexandria to his grandparents' home and attended secondary school, and it was here that his nationalist sentiment was more solidly shaped. One day, he came across an anti-British protest and decided to join; he ended up in prison with the other rioters.[6]

Nasser recounted the first demonstration in which he participated: "While crossing the Manshiya Square in Alexandria, I noticed clashes between some demonstrating students and the

---

[5] Helen Chapin Metz, ed. *Egypt: A Country Study* (Washington: GPO for the Library of Congress, 1990), 49-50.
[6] Witte, *Gamal Abdel Nasser*, 14.

police, I did not hesitate: I immediately joined the demonstrators not knowing anything about the cause of demonstration for I found no reason to ask. At the beginning it seemed that the demonstrators had the upper hand, but soon the police forces were backed with two trucks stuffed with policemen, turning the tables once more. I remember attempting to throw some stones but was immediately caught and, on trying to escape, I was struck by a blow on the head by a police baton followed by another blow until I fell down. All drenched in blood, I was driven to prison along with a group of students who failed to escape. It was at the police station, while receiving treatment for my head injuries, that I learned that the demonstration was an anti-government protest led by the 'Masr El-Fatah' (Young Egypt) society. I went to jail filled with zeal and came out fuming with anger."[7]

His father, who had always discouraged Nasser from involvement in politics, was mortified and consequently reacted harshly; he sent Nasser away from Alexandria and to a boarding school in Helwan. Yet, Nasser's experience in Alexandria would forever change him; it was in this city that Nasser, in his own words, "called out for freedom and dignity in the name of Egypt for the first time in my life."[8] Nasser's time in Alexandria became a turning point in this young revolutionary's life, as it represented his transition from an everyday protester into a zealous rebel fighting against colonialism.

It was some time before moving to Alexandria that Nasser learned of his mother's death; she had passed away after giving birth to his third brother.[9] He had been close to his mother – much closer than he was with his father – and though her death was devastating, he was also shocked that his father had kept her death a secret for months. The loss of his mother left a deep wound in his soul; he later recalled that, "my mother's death was a tragic event in itself, but losing her this way was a shock so deep that time failed to remedy…The pain and sorrow I felt back then made me think twice before hurting anyone ever since."[10] The fact that his father remarried before the year's end only added to the pain.[11]

In 1934, Nasser returned to Cairo, where his father had also relocated to, now working at a post office in the city. Nasser had never gotten along with his father, and with the loss of his mother, who had been the only connecting bridge between the two, he felt he could no longer depend on his family for moral support. He began spending more and more time outside of home, and eventually found a place with Misr al-Fatat (the Young Egypt Party), which was an extremist and ultranationalist group. He began joining, then organizing riots and demonstrations, both at his own school and at others. However, a difference in goals and opinions with the party's leadership led to Nasser dropping out by the end of the year.[12]

---

[7] Hoda Abdel Nasser, "A Historical Sketch of Gamal Abdel Nasser," *Bibliotheca Alexandria,* http://nasser.bibalex.org/Common/pictures01-%20sira_en.htm#1.
[8] Abdel Nasser, "A Historical Sketch of Gamal Abdel Nasser."
[9] Ibid., 13-14.
[10] Abdel Nasser, "A Historical Sketch of Gamal Abdel Nasser."
[11] Aburish, *Nasser: The Last Arab*, 8-9.

With no family to depend on or group to join, Nasser began focusing more and more on his studies; he pursued history and political courses and became the head of the school's student union. Additionally, he read volumes after volumes of works on revolutionaries and revolutions, from the French Revolution to Napoleon Bonaparte, Alexander the Great, Julius Caesar, and Gandhi. He even wrote a piece entitled, "Voltaire, the Man of Freedom," which was published in his school's magazine. Nasser also read Arab literature extensively, especially works on the life of the Prophet Muhammad and his companions, as well as the renowned Egyptian political leader Mustafa Kamel.[13]

Yet, Nasser was determined to continue his anti-British activities, despite his father's rebukes and protests. In November 1934, Nasser was taking part in another student protest when he was wounded in the forehead; refusing to go to the hospital for fear of arrest, Nasser ended up with a permanent three-inch crescent-shaped scar on his forehead. The protest that Nasser had participated in was sizeable, and it drew much attention; the story was run by the media, and Nasser's name was also mentioned in some newspapers. In retaliation against the protesting students, the government promptly shut down Nasser's school, then reopened it a month later. The message was clear to the British – the Egyptian people wanted full independence – and Nasser was at the forefront of this quickly growing movement.[14] He later said about the scar he received during this protest that "[the scar] will always remain a mark of honor reminding me of my national duty. That day a great number of nationalists…were assassinated and this increased my resilience to free the nation."[15]

Nasser nonetheless finished his secondary education and moved onto studying law at Fuad University. Yet, his dream of overhauling what he deemed to be a corrupt government and building a new and better one persisted; in fact, he chose to study law in university because he hoped to better understand the country's rules and regulations that kept so many in poverty. Unfortunately, Nasser was not the only one attracted by law; the legal profession was prestigious and high-earning, and Nasser was just one of thousands of young men studying law, of which a small minority would ever be able to find jobs as lawyers. After a few months of university life, disillusioned by the future that was awaiting him, Nasser dropped out of Fuad University.[16]

During the next few years, Nasser became preoccupied with politics. He joined one political group, left it, then joined another, including the Young Egypt Party, and for a short time, Hassan al-Banna's growing Muslim Brotherhood movement. In the end, he decided not to join any of these groups and parties, mostly because he never felt convinced about any of their ideologies. This experience led him to realize that there was no existing organization in Egypt that could fully achieve the goals he had in mind; in order to attain his vision of a new Egypt, he had to

[12] Ibid., 15.
[13] Abdel Nasser, "A Historical Sketch of Gamal Abdel Nasser."
[14] Aburish, *Nasser: The Last Arab*, 15.
[15] Abdel Nasser, "A Historical Sketch of Gamal Abdel Nasser."
[16] Aburish, *Nasser: The Last Arab*, 15.

create a movement himself.

Chapter 2: Nasser's Military Career

Previously, during the British occupation of Egypt, entrance into Egypt's royal military academy was an option reserved solely for Egypt's elite and middle class. However, in 1936, the ruling Wafd party that had come into power opened up the doors of the military academy in an effort to ride the anti-colonialism wave that was sweeping across the country and develop a military filled with nationalistic, politically active youth who would pave the path toward complete Egyptian independence. According to a 1936 treaty with the British, the Egyptian military, which was formerly an arm of the British occupation, became independent; plans to rapidly enlarge the army and a desperate need for new officers created new opportunities in Egypt, and the middle class youth of Nasser's generation answered this call.[17] The results were as intended – the opening up of the military academy brought together the very people who were most eager for a change in the status quo – young men of the lower classes with no stake in preserving the existing power structures.

In March 1937, Nasser's application into the royal military academy was accepted, and he began officer training as part of a cohort scheduled for an accelerated 17-month program..[18] He had never been a particularly good student, but he proved to be a better soldier; his talents were immediately recognized, and he was appointed as head of a study group within six months of entering the academy. In July of 1938, Nasser received his first appointment and was posted at Mankabad, where Anwar Sadat, his future vice president, was also sent. [19] Mankabad was a faraway outpost; it was remote, isolated, and desolate, and the loneliness of the evenings was nightly filled with long conversations around the campfire about the state of Egypt and her future. It was here in this remote outpost that the future revolutionaries first spoke of and developed plans to topple the monarchy. Together with Anwar Sadat and other junior officers, Nasser discussed his dreams and ideas for the future of Egypt, vowing to change the current state of governance.

---

[17] Joel Gordon, *Nasser: Hero of the Arab Nation* (Oxford: Oneworld Publications, 2006), 17.
[18] Ibid.
[19] Anne Alexander, *Nasser Life and Times* (London: Haus Publishing, 2005), 27.

Nasser in 1937

Nasser became especially close with Anwar Sadat, who was also the son of an impoverished laborer, and who had also turned to joining the military with dreams of achieving great change in Egypt. Sadat later recalled his first meeting with Nasser: "My impression was that he was a serious-minded youth who did not share his fellows' interest in jesting, nor would he allow anyone to be frivolous with him as this, he felt, would be an affront to his dignity. Most of my colleagues therefore kept their distance and even refrained from talking to him for fear of being misunderstood."[20] However, Sadat felt no reservations against the man who was to later become his president, and Nasser in turn found Sadat to be of the same mind, as they both agreed that a change was necessary to restore the pride of the Egyptian people and liberate the country. This marked the start of a long and fruitful friendship; little did either of them know that their friendship would shape the future of the country and impact the entire region for decades to come.

In 1939, Nasser and several other young officers, including Anwar Sadat, founded a revolutionary nationalist group they called the Free Officers Organization. Though it did not start out as the well-structured organization that it would become in the 1950s, the group was intended

---

[20] Joseph Finklestone, *Anwar Sadat: Visionary Who Dared* (London: Frank Cass Publishers, 1996), 11.

to be a loosely organized, secretive association composed of junior officers in the Egyptian army – a network of nationalist, pro-revolution soldiers, all aiming to utilize their positions in the military to topple and rebuild the Egyptian government while also ousting all foreign influence from Egypt. Sadat later recounted the six principles the group was formed to uphold: "the elimination of imperialism, the destruction of feudalism, the establishment of social justice, the formation of a strong Egyptian Army, the creation of sound democratic life, and the liberation of the government from the control of capitalists."[21]

---

[21] Ibid., 12.

Pictures of Nasser in an army uniform in 1940

Unfortunately, the group of revolutionary soldiers was broken up when its key members were assigned to different posts; Nasser was stationed in the Sudan, while Anwar Sadat was sent to Cairo.[22] The separation proved to be costly; together, they were one team and one force, but set apart, neither Nasser nor Sadat was able to instigate much change. In the following years, Nasser worked hard to continue the debates and discussions and turn ideas into action, but he failed to accomplish any real change. In fact, it was Anwar Sadat who proved to be more active. Sadat proclaimed himself leader of an anti-British revolutionary group and involved himself in many assassination and kidnapping plots. He was arrested by Egyptian authorities after being implicated in a plot involving German spies, and swiftly stripped of his rank and imprisoned.[23]

While Sadat spent his days in Cairo's prisons, by the end of 1942, Nasser had established himself as leader of the Free Officers which he sought to revive. This was the year when Nasser was transferred from his post in the Sudan to Lower Egypt, and also the year when British tanks

---

[22] Wheelock, *Nasser's New Egypt*, 4.
[23] Raymond Carroll, *Anwar Sadat* (New York: F. Watts, 1982), 21-22.

encircled the Egypt's King Farouk's Abdeen Palace and forced Farouk to yield to the installment of a Wafd-coalition government.[24] The Abdeen Palace Incident of 1942, as it has since been called, made a deep impression on Nasser, for he often referred to this day as the start of the revolution he led.[25] He later wrote about the incident that it was a blatant violation of Egyptian sovereignty, and that he was "ashamed that [the Egyptian] army has not reacted against this attack," further wishing for "calamity" to overtake the British.[26]

Throughout the next few years, Nasser worked to strengthen and organize his Free Officers. In his autobiography, Sadat recalled that "Nasser's leadership of the Free Officers' Association differed from mine. He created secret units in the army, each unknown to each other. The numbers increased daily until the organization included members in the entire armed forces, especially sensitive departments such as the army administration."[27] Thus, the organization had developed into a cell system modeled after underground Marxist groups; the membership in each cell was kept secret and unknown outside the cell itself, and members of each cell had no knowledge of the identity of the leadership. Additionally, these different cells and sections were each tasked with varying responsibilities, such as general administration, economic affairs, combat, security, terrorism, and propaganda. The economic division, for example, collected dues and was in charge of providing funds to the families of imprisoned members.[28]

In contrast to Sadat, who was heavily involved in radical activities and terror plots, Nasser and his group did little to go on the offensive. Except for the occasional meetings and sporadic distribution of pamphlets and other propaganda, the group did little to distinguish itself as a revolutionary organization aiming for a complete overhaul of the country's political structure. It did, however, develop furtive relations with other underground radical organizations, such as Hassan al-Banna's Muslim Brotherhood and Communist bodies, and this brought the Free Officers under the close surveillance of the Egyptian authorities. Several arrests were made in 1947, and the group was further forced into near inactivity. A member claimed that at this time, the group numbered over a thousand, but the more reasonable estimate made by another council member puts the figure at around ninety.[29] It was only until the 1948 Arab-Israeli War, when the government and military became occupied with the war effort, that Nasser would finally have his chance to regroup and strengthen his forces.

Chapter 3: The 1948 Arab-Israeli War

Nasser's first experience in the battlefield was in the 1948 Arab-Israeli War, which was fought between the state of Israel and an Arab coalition, formed by Egypt, Jordan, and Syria. In May

---

[24] Gabriel Warburg, "Lampson's Ultimatum to Faruq, 4 February, 1942," *Middle Eastern Studies* 11, no. 1 (1975): 24-32.
[25] Wheelock, *Nasser's New Egypt*, 6.
[26] Aburish, *Nasser: The Last Arab*, 18.
[27] Anwar El-Sadat, *Those I Have Known* (New York: Continuum, 1984), 77-78.
[28] Wheelock, *Nasser's New Egypt*, 6.
[29] Ibid., 6-7.

1948, when King Farouk ordered the Egyptian army to Palestine, Nasser was serving in the 6th Infantry Battalion.[30] Neither Nasser nor the Egyptian army was prepared for the war that would mark one of the biggest failures of the Arab coalition.

Nasser was appointed deputy commander of the Egyptian forces that secured the Faluja pocket, where thousands of Egyptian troops were besieged for months by the newly created Israeli Defense Forces. On July 12, 1948, Nasser was lightly wounded, and by August, his brigade was completely surrounded by Israeli forces; yet, Nasser's brigade refused to surrender. Diplomatic negotiations between Israel and Egypt finally led to the ceding of Faluja to Israel, and though Nasser and his troops had failed to maintain control of Faluja, they became national heroes in the eyes of much of Egypt.[31] In the end, ten months of fighting led to Arab defeat and the creation of the state of Israel, which also claimed as Israeli territory a vast stretch of Arab lands. Nasser never forgot the bitterness he felt during the four-month siege of Faluja, when the Egyptian government refused to send more troops to relieve his brigade; he began writing his book, *Philosophy of the Revolution*, during this siege.[32]

Nasser (far left) in Faluja during the war

---

[30] Muhammad Hasanayn Haykal, *The Cairo Documents: The Inside Story of Nasser and His Relationship with World Leaders, Rebels, and Statesmen* (New York: Doubleday, 1973), 103.

[31] Aburish, *Nasser: The Last Arab*, 25-26.

[32] Carol Brightman, *Total Insecurity: The Myth of American Omnipotence* (London: Verso, 2004), 233.

The war was a grand event in the lives of Nasser and his revolutionaries; it gave their project momentum, as the group deemed the war treason on the part of the Egyptian government and its allies. In the summer of 1948, the Free Officers began to organize into a more cohesive group, and by 1950, it had a central committee led by Nasser. Two major groups had an impact on Nasser and his Free Officers Movement. The first was the Muslim Brotherhood, founded by the Islamic revivalist ideologue Hassan al-Banna, who was assassinated in February of 1949. Nasser had sent emissaries to forge ties with the Muslim Brotherhood in 1948, though he had concluded that the aims and agenda of the Brotherhood diverged from his own.[33] Nonetheless, Nasser acknowledged the strong influence of the Brotherhood and the vast support it received from a large sector of Egyptian society; he thus worked to make and keep a strong alliance with the group.

The second group Nasser made contact with was the Wafd party, which was peaking in its popularity in Egypt. Notably, Nasser reached out to Ahmed Abul Fath, who was a prominent member of the Wafd and publisher of the newspaper *Al-Misri*. The alliance he made with Abul Fath proved to be advantageous, as Nasser and his group now had a media outlet through which they could voice their thoughts and ideas, which was especially useful in Nasser's early days of power as president of post-revolution Egypt.[34]

Furthermore, three events in 1949 instigated Nasser's decision to formalize his revolutionary group. The first occurred when he was appointed to be a member of a diplomatic delegation tasked with forming a ceasefire treaty with the Israelis. The experience was one that was humiliating to Nasser, who had been adamantly opposed to any kind of negotiation with Israel. The second event was more motivating; upon returning to Egypt, Nasser learned that Syria had undergone a military coup, and the civilian government had been overthrown by the Syrian armed forces. The revolution in Syria had occurred quickly and with massive support from the Syrian population. Nasser was extremely impressed and motivated by this event; he felt the same could occur in Egypt, if it had been done so successfully in neighboring Syria. Finally, the third event occurred when he was interrogated by the Egyptian Prime Minister, in front of the Army Chief of Staff, about his political activities, which had been under suspicion for some time now. Immediately after this interrogation process, Nasser made the decision to transform the loosely knit group of junior officers, supporters, and friends into a formalized association.[35]

Chapter 4: The Egyptian Revolution of 1952

The Egyptian Revolution of 1952, also known as the 23 July Revolution, transpired in an era when anti-monarchy, anti-colonialism, and anti-British sentiment were at an all-time high across Egypt, giving Nasser and his Free Officers enough impetus to implement their dream of a full-

---

[33] Ibid.

[34] Jean Lacouture, *The Demigods: Charismatic Leadership in the Third World* (New York: Knopf, 1970), 88-89.

[35] Robert Eugene Danielson, "Nasser and Pan-Arabism: Explaining Egypt's Rise in Power" (MA diss., Naval Postgraduate School, 2007), 14.

scale revolution. Even without the provocation of the Free Officers Organization, in early 1952, spontaneous riots broke out on the streets of Cairo and other major cities – evidence of the highly charged and tense environment in which the revolution eventually took place.

On January 25, 1952, British forces in the Suez Canal region took aggressive action when it ordered a police post in Ismailia to surrender for alleged support of anti-British activities. When the commander of the police post refused and mounted defenses, the British attacked, killing approximately 40 and injuring 70 Egyptian policemen.[36] Outrage spilled out onto the streets in the form of protests and riots, leading to violence, looting, and the burning down of foreign businesses in Cairo. The last straw for Nasser and his comrades was watching the riots while the Egyptian government took no action to quell the violence or retaliate against the British.

By July 1952, Nasser's units were moving into Cairo, seizing control of strategic military and government posts and encountering little resistance. Once the Free Officers had occupied most of the city, the newly created Revolutionary Command Council, which was led by Nasser and General Muhammad Naguib – Nasser's good friend and a high-ranking member of the Egyptian army – took control of the government.[37] Then, on July 23, Nasser instructed Anwar Sadat to seize control of the Cairo radio station and broadcast an official proclamation to the people announcing the coup. Sadat swiftly obliged, and the reaction on the streets to the announcement of the coup was mixed; though many were overjoyed by the toppling of the British-controlled government, they did not know what was to replace the old system of rule, and whether it would be any more or less beneficial to the people of Egypt. As Sadat later described, there was a "festive silence" in the streets of Egypt's cities that day.[38]

Nasser then asked Sadat to communicate to King Farouk the terms of the ultimatum the Free Officers Movement was presenting – either the king could leave Egypt, or he could suffer the consequences deemed fit by the rebels. Unsurprisingly, King Farouk chose a swift departure; on July 26, 1952, the last king of Egypt left his country for exile in Italy.[39] The revolution that Nasser and his fellow fighters had all dreamed about had finally become a reality.

The revolution thus unfolded surprisingly quickly, with the abdication and exile of King Farouk achieved in a mere few days. A small band of low-ranking officers, who had initiated a coup with no professed desire to govern, had become within the brief span of a few months rulers of their country. Though the overthrow of the king had been the initial and primary goal of the revolution, the Free Officers quickly moved to achieve further political goals, including abolishing the constitutional monarchy and the high status of the Egyptian aristocracy, establishing the Republic of Egypt, ending the British occupation of Egypt, and securing the

---

[36] Aburish, *Nasser: The Last Arab*, 35.
[37] Danielson, "Nasser and Pan-Arabism: Explaining Egypt's Rise in Power," 15.
[38] Ibid., 33.
[39] Amina Elbendary, "The Long Revolution," *Al-Ahram,* July 18, 2002,
    http://weekly.ahram.org.eg/2002/595/sc2.htm.

independence of neighboring Sudan, which had also been under the control of the British. The new revolutionary government adopted a staunchly nationalist agenda, ushering in the spread of what came to be known as Arab nationalism, or Nasserism – an ideological movement comprising components of anti-imperialism, pan-Arabism, nationalism, and Arab socialism. The results of the revolution were not constrained to the borders of Egypt; Nasserism was exported to other countries as "a psychological phenomenon shared by an entire Arab generation." Nasserism was less an ideological movement the likes of Marxism or Leninism, and more an "attitude of mind" that had appealed to and spread across other Arab countries, giving them a feeling of confidence in themselves, largely counterbalancing the psychological shock of the loss of Palestine in 1948.[40]

For such a dramatic and impactful revolution that completely reshaped Egypt, it lasted no more than three days, and was conducted by no more than a hundred junior-ranking officers of the army. The swiftness and the ease with which the Free Officers succeeded were the results of various pieces of the revolution perfectly falling into place: the rapid reorganization and restructuring of the Free Officers by Nasser in the early 1950s; the increasing woes of the Egyptian people and burgeoning discontent for the deteriorating political and economic order; the anger and humiliation felt by the nation from the defeat in the 1948 war with Israel; and the lack of a strong state-controlled military that could be effectively mobilized against an oncoming force from within.[41] In addition, Nasser had made certain that King Farouk would receive no aid from the king's foreign allies; he had notified the U.S. and British governments of his intentions, and both had agreed in a change of power.[42]

The Free Officers did not intend to install themselves in the new government, at least initially; they merely sought to build a stable and truly democratic parliamentary government. In fact, it has been written that Nasser himself did not believe that as a low-ranking junior officer, he was qualified to lead or that he would be accepted by the Egyptian people as the new leader of Egypt. As such, the higher ranking and more prominent officer, General Muhammad Naguib, was selected to be the leader of the revolution and the subsequent rebuilding of Egypt, at least in name. Nasser removed himself from the spotlight and took more of a backstage role, as he believed that the military was the "guardians of the people's interests" against the monarchy and the elite class, while the day-to-day tasks of state governance should be left to civilians.[43]

Chapter 5: The Egyptian Republic

On June 18, 1953, the Egyptian monarchy was officially abolished, and the Republic of Egypt

---

[40] Elie Podeh and Onn Winckler, "Introduction: Nasserism as a Form of Populism," in *Rethinking Nasserism: Revolution and Historical Memory in Modern Egypt*, ed. Elie Podeh and Onn Winckler (Gainesville, FL: University Press of Florida, 2004), 2-3.
[41] Joel Gordon, *Nasser's Blessed Movement: Egypt's Free Officers and the July Revolution* (New York: Oxford University Press, 1992), 39.
[42] Aburish, *Nasser: The Last Arab*, 35-39.
[43] Ibid., 41.

declared, with General Naguib as its first president.[44] Ali Maher, who was the former prime minister during Farouk's reign and a veteran politician, was reappointed to his previous position and tasked with forming an all-civilian cabinet. Maher had also served as somewhat of a mentor and advisor to King Farouk, and was well known for his anti-British sentiments. The Free Officers, on the other hand, maintained its position in power as the Revolutionary Command Council, with General Naguib as chairman and Nasser as vice-chairman. Historian Jean Lacouture wrote of Nasser's initial reservations about presenting himself as a leading figure to the Egyptian public that: "[Nasser's] first steps certainly gave no hint that a Bonaparte had come on stage. Nasser was the brains of the movement, but there was no evidence that he planned to take it over." [45]

Lacouture further wrote about Nasser's personality and style of leadership: "All we know about this period of Nasser's career comes from his friends, Saroit Okacha, Anouar el-Sadat, and Ahmed Abul Fath. Fath, who began to oppose [Nasser] more openly two years later, is the only one to suggest that Gamal was permeable to personal ambition. Every other record seems to imply the opposite: *Bikhachi* (Lieutenant Colonel) Nasser, an excellent instructor in tactics at the military academy of Abassiah, organizer of the Doubat el Ahrar (Free Officers) conspiracy, was respected by his friends and considered a rank-and-file leader, not a 'boss.' He was influential rather than imposing. He argued and tried to persuade, disregarding his rank and privilege."[46]

---

[44] Ibid., 35-39.
[45] Jean Lacouture, *The Demigods: Charismatic Leadership in the Third World,* 90.
[46] Ibid., 92.

Nasser (seated) and other members of the Free Officers in 1953

Sulayman al-Hafez, Muhammad Naguib, and Nasser after deposing Farouk

Relations between Nasser's Revolutionary Command Council and Ali Maher gradually grew tense, then deteriorated. Maher clashed with Nasser and his supporters frequently over Nasser's domestic policies, including the agrarian reform and the reorganization of political parties; Maher felt that Nasser's schemes were far too radical and conservative, out of place in a self-professed nascent democracy. Maher soon resigned, citing his reasons as insurmountable differences with the council.[47] In Maher's stead, Major General Muhammad Naguib assumed the role of prime minister in addition to the presidency. Nasser was declared deputy premier and interior minister, though in truth, as the one with all the power and influence, he was already by this point the true leader of the republic of Egypt.[48]

Soon after, an anti-government plot – formed by some of the old politicians who had been stripped of much of their pre-revolution powers, working in conjunction with several ambitious army officers – was discovered. The response that Nasser and the Revolutionary Command Council took to this first instance of treasonous activity was swift and severe. All those suspected of involvement in the plot were arrested and the officers court martialed, and the council assumed all legislative and executive power for the next three years.[49]

[47] Amina Elbendary, "The Long Revolution."
[48] Elbendary, "The Long Revolution."
[49] Raymond Carroll, *Anwar Sadat* (New York: F. Watts, 1982), 36.

Nasser further implemented policies to centralize power within the presidency and outlaw any and all social and political parties that challenged his rule or posed a threat to his presidency. Nasser and his supporters began establishing their own political party, which was to become the ruling Arab Socialist Union (ASU). On January 16, 1953, the Revolutionary Command Council also dissolved and banned all political parties in the country, and the radical Islamic revivalist party, the Muslim Brotherhood, was also outlawed and forced underground.

By the end of the year, the nascent revolutionary regime could already point to some proud accomplishments. Prior to the revolution, less than 6% of Egyptians owned more than 65% of the land in Egypt, while less than 0.5% of Egyptians owned more than one-third of all fertile land.[50] The 1952 Agrarian Reform Law began the process of a major land redistribution program to rectify the centralization of land ownership in the hands of the wealthy, limiting land ownership to around 200 acres and distributing previously unobtainable plots of land to landless farmers. In addition, the property of the royal family was confiscated, and the money was used to build hospitals and schools in rural areas and fund infrastructure projects.[51] Politicians and officials of the old regime were swiftly tried and sentenced by a revolutionary tribunal.[52] It appeared the new republic was well on its way to development and growth.

Possibly the biggest accomplishment for Nasser and his regime was the signing of the Anglo-Egyptian Evacuation Agreement on October 19, 1954. After Egypt's independence from the British in 1922, and even after the revolution and the ouster of the king, British troops and advisors had remained in the country. By 1954, the revolutionary leaders could no longer stall one of the major objectives of the revolution – the complete ouster of British intervention and influence from Egypt. Nasser thus embarked on negotiations for the withdrawal of all British troops. The British submitted their terms – they wished to maintain their hold on the Suez Canal base for another 24 months, then retain some of their stores and about 1,200 civilian experts in Egypt for the next seven years. The council agreed, and the draft was accepted. The last British soldier left Egyptian soil on June 19, 1956, and the revolutionary government was finally able to herald the end of the British occupation of Egypt.[53]

[50] Tarek Osman, *Egypt on the Brink* (New Haven: Yale University Press, 2010), 45.
[51] Carroll, *Anwar Sadat,* 38.
[52] Elbendary, "The Long Revolution."
[53] Alagna, *Anwar Sadat,* 44.

President Muhammad Naguib and Prime Minister Nasser in 1954

Chapter 6: President Nasser

Although sovereign power was technically held by General Muhammad Naguib, "in order to protect the revolution," true power was actually in the hands of Nasser. In fact, the Revolutionary Command Council itself once explained the reasons behind putting Naguib at the forefront while keeping Nasser and much of the other true power holders in the shadows. In a statement to the citizens of Egypt, the council wrote, "From the very beginning, the Revolution faced considerable hardships which were decisively tackled without tending to personal interests – that is why it has been firmly established and is steadily moving towards its goals. [The Revolutionary Command Council is] certain that you know the extent of the hardships faced by the Revolution…This heavy load was carried by the members of the Council whose motive was to take the nation to a safe shore, however much it cost them. What made matters worse is the fact that the Council members decided to nominate a leader for the Revolution who was not one of its members, as they were all young men. Major General Mohammed Naguib was chosen, who was much older and held a higher rank, had a good reputation and was not polluted with the corruption that prevailed at that time."[54]

Naguib therefore had more authority and enjoyed greater respect from the people, due to his high rank and his stellar military record and political reputation. He was the perfect face of the government while Nasser worked in the shadows, keeping himself locked up in his private office, commanding the furtive meetings of the Revolutionary Command Council. Throughout this period of ruling a country while entrenched in the shadows, Nasser consistently gave the impression that he was greatly attracted to, yet greatly fearful of, responsibility. Power enticed him, yet he also cringed at the thought of attaining it.

Anwar Sadat, Nasser's future vice president and later his successor, has written extensively about Nasser's fickle personality centered on paranoia and mistrust. Nasser was inherently a deeply suspicious man, often lending an ear to rumors and gossip, not knowing such stories might have been contrived by the very person who was feeding him the information; as Sadat recalled, Nasser was "the eternal doubter, cautious, full of bitterness, high-strung."[55]

In his biography of Nasser, Robert St. John chose "The Reluctant Dictator" as one chapter title – befitting of Nasser's first few years in power. Not until several months after the July 1952 coup did Nasser authorize the publishing of his name as the new regime's key member.[56] The historian Jean Lacouture has described Nasser in his initial years of power as "a straightforward and rather awkward fellow, somewhat round-shouldered, with a piercing and mournful gaze, sunburned, laconic, and unassuming."[57]

By June of 1953, it was public knowledge that Gamal Abdel Nasser was the true holder of the reins of power in the Egyptian government. Naguib was still president and prime minister, but "people whispered that the 'Good General' was only the Colonel's color bearer."[58] As the leader of the Revolutionary Command Council and Minister of Interior, Nasser was responsible for much, if not all, of state governance, and with the secret police also under his control, he had amassed near total concentration of power.

Nasser's consolidation of power was not limited to his own party and group; he set out to crush any opposition parties that could threaten his rule. Throughout 1953, Nasser's regime rode down any and all political opposition, suppressing parties that had once been the most popular in Egypt, like the Wafd party and the Muslim Brotherhood, imprisoning their leaders and key figures, and even sentencing a number of them to death. When the Brotherhood set out to contest Nasser's dictatorship and organize demonstrations at Cairo University, it was crushed by Nasser's forces, as thousands of protest participants were placed under arrest.[59]

---

[54] Abdel Nasser, "A Historical Sketch of President Gamal Abdel-Nasser."
[55] El-Sadat, *Those I Have Known,* 79.
[56] Jean Lacouture, *The Demigods: Charismatic Leadership in the Third World,* 93.
[57] Ibid., 94.
[58] Ibid., 99.
[59] Ibid., 99-100.

In February 1954, General Muhammad Naguib offered his resignation, citing insurmountable disputes with members of the Revolutionary Command Council as his reasons for stepping down. The council initially accepted Naguib's resignation and appointed Nasser to replace him, but protesters gathered in the streets, calling for Naguib's reinstatement. Though the council yielded to the demonstrations and reinstated Naguib by March, the rift was already established and growing between Naguib and Nasser.

On April 17, 1954, Nasser was nominated as prime minister, while Naguib remained as president – that is, until October 26, 1954, when a member of the Muslim Brotherhood attempted to assassinate Nasser while he was giving a speech in Alexandria. Though Nasser was unharmed, Naguib was implicated in the plot, as evidence emerged that Naguib had been in contact with the Muslim Brotherhood and even promised to support the group in case they managed to overthrow the existing regime. Naguib was removed, and Nasser took charge.[60]

Nasser in Alexandria a day after the assassination attempt

In early 1956, Nasser announced a new constitution, setting up a presidential system of

---

[60] Abdel Nasser, "A Historical Sketch of President Gamal Abdel-Nasser."

government. Several months later, in June 1956, Nasser was elected president of Egypt in a national plebiscite. Consequently, the three-year rule of the Revolutionary Council ended, and the council was dissolved, in acknowledgement of the transition to civilian rule.[61] A single party system was established under the National Union party, a movement Nasser described as "the cadre through which we will realize our revolution."[62] To him, the revolution was far from over – not until he could develop Egypt into the modern and leading nation of his visions.

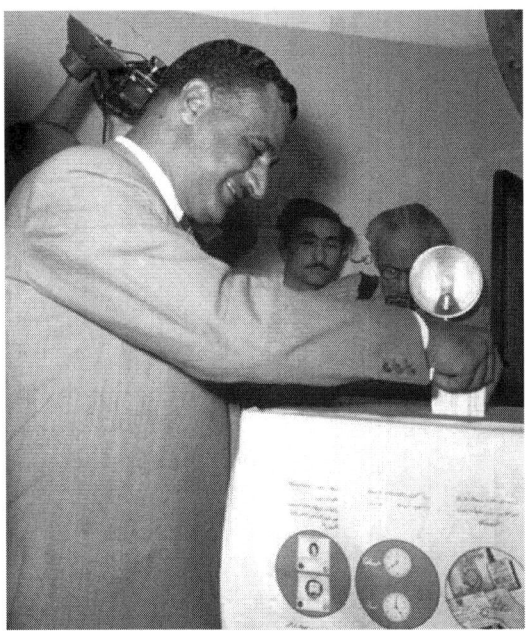

A picture of Nasser voting in June 1956

Chapter 7: Pan-Arabism

Pan-Arabism, also referred to as Arab Nationalism, flourished across the Middle East during the mid-twentieth century, and Gamal Abdel Nasser had much to do with this phenomenon. It must be noted first that no one scholar has come to a consensus about what pan-Arabism is or what exactly it embodies; some believe it to represent the creation of a single Arab state, while others see it as signifying "the idea that the Arabs are people linked by special bonds of language, history and religion, and that their political organization should in some way reflect this reality."[63] Whether the terms is used symbolically, politically, culturally, or ideologically,

---

[61] Ibid., 46.
[62] Alexander, *Nasser Life and Times*, 126.

pan-Arabism does capture a certain unity and bond among the Arab states in the Middle East – that all Arabs are connected through common culture and roots in identity, and that this connection should lead to intra-Arab cooperation in the political arena as well. As prominent scholar of the Middle East Bernard Lewis wrote, "a nation denotes a group of people held together by a common language, belief in descent, and in a shared history and destiny."[64] The concept of pan-Arabism revolved around this idea – connecting Arab culture and history to the politics and policies of the various Arab countries.

Scholars differ in their views on precisely when and where pan-Arabism began. However, most agree that the decolonization of much of the Middle East region in the early and mid-1900s led to the creation of an ideological and political vacuum, resulting in the weakening of the population's culture and sense of identity. Scholar Rashid Khalidi has written that much of this weakness was created by the fragmentation of the Arab world by foreign imperialist powers that portioned off and claimed control over varying countries in the region, solely to serve their own interests, without care for preserving regional unity.[65] In fact, European imperialists placed great focus on keeping the Arab states divided and apart, in fear of their uniting and ultimately threatening their political and economic interests. Thus, when the region rapidly decolonized and regained independence, it makes sense then that the population felt the sudden need to unite and connect with something to provide them a sense of identity. For the first time since the Ottoman Empire, with the end of colonial rule, the Arabs were able to reflect on what it means to be Arab and what it means to live in an Arab country.

Though it is absolutely true that Nasser championed the pan-Arabism cause, both in his own country and across the Middle East, it must be noted that pan-Arabism was in actuality already a significant part of Egyptian society prior to Nasser's ascendancy to power in the 1950s. Most scholars agree that pan-Arabism emerged in Egypt sometime around the late 1920s and early 1930s. Scholar Ralph M. Coury identifies the Egyptian ruling class during these times as responsible for this emergence of pan-Arabism; he argues that much of the ruling class was becoming more and more focused on Arab unity and cooperation among different branches and sectors of the Egyptian ruling class, and that this transition for greater cohesiveness was reflected in the political and socioeconomic developments in the country.[66] Pan-Arabism emerged and developed earlier in Egypt than in other countries of the region because of the ruling class's propensity to cooperate, and their ability to use this to their advantage to spread the ideals of pan-

[63] Rashid Khalidi, *The Origins of Arab Nationalism: Introduction in The Origins of Arab Nationalism,* ed. Rashid Khalidi, Lisa Anderson, Muhammad Muslih, and Reeva S. Simon (New York: Columbia University Press, 1991), vii.

[64] Adeed Dawisha, *Arab Nationalism in the Twentieth Century: From Triumph to Despair* (Princeton: Princeton University Press, 2003), 6, quoting Bernard Lewis, The Multiple Identities of the Middle East (New York: Schocken Books, 1998), 81.

[65] Rashid Khalidi, "Arab Nationalism: Historical Problems in the Literature," *The American Historical Review* 96, no. 5 (December 1991), 1366.

[66] Ralph M. Coury, "Who "Invented Egyptian Arab Nationalism? Part 2," *International Journal of Middle East Studies* 14, no. 4 (November 1982), 459.

Arabism by strengthening economic and cultural ties with other countries in the Middle East.[67]

Thus, Egypt was looked upon as a leader in the pan-Arabism cause by many of the other countries and populations of the region, particularly as Egypt struggled against European imperialism throughout the early 1900s. Many Arabs felt that Egypt could lead and aid them in their own struggles against the effects of imperialism and Western colonization. Even the secular Egyptian Communist Party, which is decidedly focused on ideology more than ethnicity or religion, added a clause in its party program in 1931, "calling for struggle on behalf of all Arab peoples from imperialism, as well as the achievement of a complete Arab unity that included all free Arabs."[68] This idea of Egypt as the leader of the Arab world and pan-Arabism developed, then strengthened during the presidency of Nasser.

Nasser proved to be one of the most important leaders in the region who was able to popularize the idea of Arab nationalism. He recognized the advantages Egypt had with its large size and population, as well as strategic geographic location and political importance in the Arab world, and thus worked to spread his idea of pan-Arabism across Egypt and the region. As scholar Israel Gershoni noted, "Egypt's unique virtues, geopolitical features, cultural advantages, and spiritual and religious power destine[d] Egypt to bear the crown of all Arab leadership and oblige[d] it to fulfill its pan-Arab mission."[69] To Nasser, pan-Arabism was more than an ideology or a united identity; he viewed it as an opportunity to politically and culturally influence other countries in the Middle East.

Nasser's realization of the potential of pan-Arabism, and his decision to adopt it as a political strategy, can be seen in much of Nasser's speeches and public rhetoric during the 1950s and 1960s. In addresses, he consistently referred to Egypt as an Arab country, Arab Egypt, or a member nation of the Arab world. For example, in the memorable July 1954 radio address he gave during the first anniversary of the launching of the prominent Egyptian transnational radio program, *Voice of the Arabs*, Nasser referred to all Arabs as being "one nation" and identified Egypt as part and parcel of that united Arab nation.[70] Furthermore, in the national charter he authored in 1962, Nasser referred to Egyptians as "Arab people of Egypt" and asserted that "there is no conflict whatsoever between Egyptian patriotism and Arab nationalism."[71] As such, the idea that Egypt was part of a larger Arab entity, and that other Arab nations were also part of this same united entity, was greatly furthered by Nasser. Through his fiery speeches, addresses, and announcements, he continued to drill into the minds of not only his people but also the Arab population the idea that Arab unity and cooperation were absolutely necessary to defend all the

---

[67] Ibid.
[68] Ibid., 464.
[69] Israel Gershoni, *The Emergence of Pan-Arabism in Egypt* (Israel: Tel Aviv University, 1981), 74.
[70] James Jankowski, *Nasser's Egypt, Arab Nationalism, and the United Arab Republic* (Colorado: Lynne Rienner Publishers, 2002), 60.
[71] James Jankowski, *Arab Nationalism in "Nasserism" and Egyptian State Policy, 1952-1958 in Rethinking Nationalism in the Arab Middle East*, ed. James Jankowski and Israel Gershoni (New York: Columbia University Press, 1997), 151.

countries of the region against the Western powers and Israeli aggression. In a July 1957 speech, Nasser fervently described Arab nationalism as "a weapon for every Arab state…employed against aggression," and further stated that "it is necessary for the aggressor to know that, if he aggresses against my Arab country, he will endanger his interests."[72]

Nasser was able to successfully use the broad support and widespread popularity he received from these statements to boost and expand Egypt's role in the politics of the Middle East. Furthermore, Nasser understood that in order for Egypt to fulfill its role as leader of the Arab world, as prescribed by pan-Arabism, he must first have a stable nation with strong domestic policies before he could turn his attention to positioning Egypt in intra-Arab politics. This can be seen by looking at both the domestic and foreign policies of Nasser during his presidency, which will be examined further below.

Chapter 8: The Suez Crisis

The 1950s were the times of the Cold War, when there was growing animosity between the U.S. and the Soviet Union. As Nasser maneuvered through the dangerous game of nation-building in a world dominated by the political, economic, and military rivalry of the two superpowers, Nasser's government quickly became the model of non-alignment, as Cairo refused to side concretely with either power. Egypt came to represent the voices of the undeveloped, underdeveloped, and post-colonial nations of the world, which wished to stay free of the expanding U.S.-Soviet rift and the developing Cold War.

The British, on the other hand, had left Egypt relatively peacefully, however reluctantly; Egypt was a geographically, economically, and politically strategic country in the oil-rich Middle East, and thus, London was by no means satisfied with its loss of influence in the country. In order to retain Britain's control over this region, in 1955, then British Prime Minister Anthony Eden initiated discussions for the creation of what became known as the Baghdad Pact, designed to create an alliance with pro-Western states in the Middle East. Countries that were eager to join the pact included Iraq, Turkey, Iran, and Pakistan, which were anxious to strengthen their defenses during a time when the Soviet Union's infiltration into the Middle East was a very real threat. On the other hand, Nasser was infuriated by what he deemed a growing Western aggression into the politics of the Middle East, and much of Egypt also voiced their strong opposition to the Baghdad Pact. Representing his people's voices, Nasser gave fiery speeches criticizing the British, which was broadcasted by the transnational Voice of Arabs radio station in Cairo. Nasser enjoyed immense popular support in neighboring states due to his strong stance against the Baghdad pact, and this led to other Arab countries, most notably Syria and Jordan, criticizing and refuting the pact as well.[73]

---

[72] Ibid., 155.

[73] Gerald Butt, "Lesson From History: 1955 Baghdad Pact," *BBC News*, February 26, 2003, http://news.bbc.co.uk/2/hi/middle_east/2801487.stm.

Egypt's open criticisms and strong opposition against the pact angered not only Britain, but also its ally, the United States. When Egypt proposed a weapons deal with the U.S., hoping for a strictly financial deal, it discovered that the U.S. was only interested in political alliances; Washington offered its weapons at no cost, in exchange for Egyptian loyalty and an American presence in Egypt. However, Nasser had no intention of placing Egypt under the influence and control of a Western power so soon after it had finally liberated itself from Britain. Though an arms deal with the Soviet Union also initially fell through, in 1955, Soviet Premier Nikita Khrushchev finally signed a deal, cementing military ties between Cairo and Moscow.[74] By 1957, Egypt received Soviet tanks, jets, and other arms and weapons worth approximately $150 million, and between 1955 and 1966, the arms deals between the two nations continued, totaling approximately $1.19 billion.[75]

Egypt's most important trial as a newly established republic, and as beacon of the post-colonial non-alignment countries, came in 1956. This was when the much-anticipated Aswan High Dam project was underway, and many Western countries and international organizations, such as the U.S., France, Britain, and the World Bank, had agreed to help finance it, promising funds of approximately $70 million.[76] The dam project was key to Nasser's plans for Egypt's growing economy; it would improve irrigation greatly, allowing more crops to be grown and harvested and bettering the lives of thousands of farmers in Egypt. However, Nasser soon discovered that his rejection of the weapons deal with the U.S. and the 1955 arms deal with the Soviets had irked the U.S.; though Egypt had been strictly looking to build up its defenses, and not necessarily attempting to establish political and military ties with the Soviet Union, the U.S. viewed the deal as Egypt choosing a side. Additionally, the tension between Egypt and the U.S. had been building up for some time now; Americans had gritted their teeth as Nasser adopted a series of anti-West positions, including the recognition of Communist China and assisting Algerian rebels against the French. The U.S. subsequently retaliated by calling on its allies to back out of the dam project, effectively withholding the money needed to complete it.[77] The Soviet Union saw its chance to strengthen its ties with Egypt and swiftly offered to finance the High Dam project, further earning the ire of the Western states, but boosting Nasser's confidence and Egypt's morale.

On July 26, 1956, in one of the most historic speeches that stunned the nation and the world, Nasser announced the nationalization of the Suez Canal. By doing this, Nasser was not only emphasizing Egyptian independence and political might, but also creating another source of tax revenue for the country, which would ultimately be used for the Aswan High Dam project and other social and infrastructure projects. The move was unprecedented and thought impossible, as

---

[74] Ibid., 39.

[75] Ali M. Yahya, *Egypt and the Soviet Union, 1952-1972: A Study in the Power of the Small State* (PhD diss., University Microfilms International, Indiana University, 1981), 140-142.

[76] Elbendary, "The Long Revolution."

[77] Alagna, *Anwar Sadat,* 46.

the canal was built and owned by a British and French consortium; yet, Nasser gave no care and declared the canal to be the property of Egypt. Though many of his advisors expressed their doubts with this abrupt maneuver to nationalize one of the most economically significant canals in the world, the Egyptian people were in full support of Nasser; his popularity skyrocketed as a result.

A picture of Nasser helping to raise a flag near the Suez Canal

The nationalization announcement was greeted with much enthusiasm and emotion by the rest of the Arab world as well. Political scientist Mahmoud Hamad wrote that it was only after the Suez Canal's nationalization that Nasser gained near-total popular legitimacy ad firmly placed himself as the "spokesman for the masses not only in Egypt, but all over the Third World."[78] However, Nasser's sudden move was viewed as an abrupt slap against the countries it held economic and political treaties with. In October of 1956, Britain, France, and Israel struck Egypt simultaneously – Israel from the ground, and Britain and French from the air – seizing key bases in the Sinai, and in one swift sweep, bombarding all the aircraft that Egypt had bought from the

---

[78] Mahmoud Hamad, "When the Gavel Speaks: Judicial Politics in Modern Egypt (PhD diss., University of Utah, 2008). 96.

Soviets.[79] Egypt hastily asked for aid from the Soviet Union, which pointedly refused.

Aid finally came not from the Soviet Union, nor from neighboring Arab countries, but from the most unexpected country – the United States. Angered by the fact that the leader of the democratic bloc and Western alliance had not been forewarned about this tripartite aggression, and deeply affronted by the unilateralism of his European allies, U.S. President Dwight D. Eisenhower demanded that the three countries immediately halt their advance and withdraw their troops. Britain, France, and Israel – just as surprised about the forcefulness of the U.S. as Egypt was – had no choice but to comply. Egypt emerged largely unscathed and won full control of the Suez Canal – though without the intervention of the U.S., it would have certainly been defeated. As a result of this crisis, Nasser implemented a set of laws and regulations imposing very rigorous requirements for residency and citizenship for Egyptians, as well as forced expulsions, which mostly affected foreign nationals and Egyptian Jews.[80]

On April 8, the Suez Canal was finally reopened, and Nasser's political position was enhanced by the failure of the tripartite invasion, which was largely seen by the world as an attempt to topple Nasser and his government. The crisis gave Nasser instant credibility and earned great popularity and support for Egypt throughout the Arab countries. Leaders of countries across the region sent letters of support and congratulations to Egypt, and "even the Council of the League of Arab States declared the solidarity of Arab governments with Egypt."[81] Egypt was lifted to a leadership role in the politics of the region, as it had accomplished something that no other country in the region had been able to do; it had defied not one Western power, but a coalition of three. The Egyptian victory resulted in Egypt, Syria, Jordan, and Saudi Arabia signing a new treaty, the Arab Solidarity Pact, in 1957, which reaffirmed their commitment to intra-Arab cooperation and regional security.[82]

Chapter 9: The United Arab Republic

By the late 1950s, pan-Arabism was the dominant ideology of the Arab world, with Nasser at the forefront. Historian and scholar Adeed Dawisha credited Nasser's rising status as the undisputed leader of Arab nationalism to his "charisma, bolstered by his perceived victory in the Suez Crisis" – perceived because it was more an American victory than an Egyptian one.[83] Nonetheless, Nasser's ideas of Arab unity had at this point spread all across the Middle East, gaining the support of not just the population of Arab countries, but also regional civilian organizations, political groups, and heads of state. His followers began calling themselves Nasserites, despite Nasser's objections to the use of the term.[84]

---

[79] Carroll, *Anwar Sadat,* 47.
[80] Joel Benin, *The Dispersion of Egyptian Jewry: Culture, Politics, and the Formation of a Modern Diaspora* (Cairo: American University in Cairo Press, 2005), 87.
[81] Jankowski, *Nasser's Egypt, Arab Nationalism, and the United Arab Republic,* 83.
[82] Ibid., 87.
[83] Dawisha, *Arab Nationalism in the Twentieth Century: From Triumph to Despair*, 184.
[84] Aburish, *Nasser: The Last Arab*, 135-136.

Yet, despite his popularity with the people, in terms of regional politics, Nasser could only depend on Syria as its stalwart ally, partly because of their geographic proximity but also because the two governments had historically enjoyed strong and cooperative ties. In September of 1957, Turkish troops mobilized along the Syrian-Turkish border, breeding rumors that the countries of the Baghdad Pact, led by the United States, were planning to attack and topple Syria's leftist government.[85] In response, Syria requested Egyptian aid, and Nasser sent a contingent force to Syria as a display of solidarity. The move further boosted Nasser's position as leader of the Arab world and elevated his popularity, especially in Syria.

As instability continued to spread across Syria, Nasser received Syrian delegations seeking immediate unification with Egypt. Initially, Nasser was skeptical of the idea; as much of a proponent of pan-Arabism as he was, he did not believe pan-Arabism meant the complete political unification of Arab countries, but rather, cooperation to achieve mutual political, economic, and social goals. He also cited the two countries' incompatible economies and political governance structures, the Syrian military's history of intervention in government affairs, and the seemingly unsolvable factionalism of Syria's political parties as reasons for his rejection.[86] Additionally, Nasser reportedly told a Lebanese journalist that "any unity project among Arab states would be met with vigorous resistance by the British and the Americans, and even the Soviet Union might not be agreeable to such an idea."[87] Thus, though Nasser was a fervent Arab nationalist and supporter of the pan-Arab cause, he was also a realist who saw that such a unity project may draw the ire and possible resistance of foreign powers.

However, in January 1958, a Syrian delegation, sent by the ruling Baathist Party in Syria, finally managed to convince Nasser of an impending takeover of the Syrian government by communist forces and the need for unification to prevent it. On February 1, 1958, the United Arab Republic (UAR) was formed, with Nasser as president of the Egyptian-Syrian union. The announcement took much of the Arab world by surprise; according to historian Adeed Dawisha: "[The formation of the UAR] came as a stunning surprise to most Arabs and non-Arabs. No one whose expectations were shaped by rational assessment could think that an organic unity between two Arab states was at all possible in such a short space of time. It was not the actual unity that was so surprising; Arab nationalists fervently believed in the *eventual* amalgamation of Arab countries. But no one…was prepared for the breathless pace at which events were to unfold."[88]

Nasser installed himself as the sole leader of the UAR and immediately set out to crush communism in Syria, starting by dismissing many Communists from government posts.[89] He further established a new constitution and proclaimed the creation of a 600-member National

[85] Dawisha, *Arab Nationalism in the Twentieth Century: From Triumph to Despair*, 191-192.
[86] Ibid., 193.
[87] Ibid., 187.
[88] Ibid., 186.
[89] Aburish, *Nasser: The Last Arab*, 150-151.

Assembly, with 400 members from Egypt and 200 from Syria, as well as ordering the dissolution of all political parties. Furthermore, Nasser appointed vice presidents for each province – Sabri al-Asali in the Egyptian province and Akram al-Hawrani in the Syrian province.[90]

The union proved to be short-lived, and a large factor contributing to its dissolution was the form in which the UAR emerged, which had not been what the Syrian Baathists had envisioned. Nasser, as the one being approached to form a union, was able to request and achieve a number of conditions for union, and one of the most significant ones was for the two countries to be completely integrated, not just federated as the Syrians initially proposed. However, because of this union and the position Nasser held as undisputed leader of the UAR, Syria soon found itself dominated by the stronger, more populous, and more efficient Egypt. The UAR's Provisional Constitution of 1958 called for double the number of Egyptian parliamentarians then Syrian ones. The first UAR cabinet included 14 Syrians out of 34 members, all of them leading politicians and military figures whom Nasser wanted removed from their bases of power.[91] As previously mentioned, the Communist party was oppressed and all political parties were dissolved; any and all rivals of the government were now driven underground and powerless. But the Syrian Baathists did not find themselves in the favored position they expected, as they soon discovered that the UAR was completely run solely by Nasser, in a form akin to dictatorship.

Opposition to the union quickly mounted among the Syrian political officials and elite. Although a number of nationalization, modernization, and land reform measures had been implemented in Syria, its people were increasingly dissatisfied with Egypt's domination. For example, Egyptians took control of many of the important administrative posts in Syria, and Syrian army officers were transferred to Egypt while Egyptians took key military posts in Syria. A prolonged drought made matters worse in Syria, as an exacerbating economic crisis brought about social and political unrest.[92] Despite the deteriorating situation, Nasser made little effort to placate Syrian dissatisfaction and continued with his planned integration of the UAR. On September 28, 1961, secessionist Syrian army units orchestrated a coup in Damascus, ensuing in a rapid power transition; Syria seceded from the UAR soon thereafter.

Chapter 10: The Six-Day War

The final momentous event of Nasser's presidency was the 1967 Six Day War, fought between Israel and a coalition of Arab states, including Egypt. The great debacle that this war would bring about for Nasser, Egypt, and the Arab World would impact Nasser's presidency greatly.

The commander-in-chief of the Egyptian forces was Field Marshal Abdel Hakim Amer, who was a good friend of Nasser's, and who had rose within the ranks of the military largely due to his friendship with the president. Amer was known to be greedy, power-hungry, and willing to

---

[90] Ibid., 161-162.
[91] "United Arab Republic," http://countrystudies.us/syria/14.htm.
[92] Ibid.

go beyond rules and regulations to achieve his goals. For example, in 1965, Nasser discovered that Amer and his subordinates had been using unlawful and brutal methods of interrogation and detention against members of the Muslim Brotherhood, and even against those who had nothing to do with the Brotherhood, but were merely "suspected" of involvement in the banned Islamist organization. Many of his advisors urged Nasser to remove Amer from his post, but Nasser was unable to act against his friend or see the dangers of keeping such a man in a high post.[93] This was who the Egyptian armed forces were being led by as war with Israel began to loom in the late 1960s.

Nasser and Sadat in 1964

---

[93] Carroll, *Anwar Sadat,* 51.

A picture of Nasser being sworn in for a second term in 1965

Israel was expanding into Arab territories, forcing Arab countries to go on the defensive to protect their territories. When in late 1966, Israel began engaging Jordanian troops in sporadic clashes, Nasser came under strong pressure from other Arab states to join in the increasing hostilities against Israel. Arab states urged Nasser to close the Strait of Tiran – Israel's only outlet to international waters. Boosted by rising popular expectations of Arab, and particularly Egyptian, military might, on May 18, 1967, Nasser demanded the withdrawal of the United Nations Emergency Force (UNEF) stationed in Egypt's side of its border with Israel in the Sinai Peninsula, then ordered Egyptian forces into the Sinai at the pretext of protecting its sovereign territory from a coming threat. The Straits of Tiran was closed, and Egypt signed a defense pact with Jordan and Syria.[94]

It has been analyzed that Nasser was likely not seeking an open war or direct conflict with Israel. Though Egypt had considerably strengthened its forces since the revolution, much of its troops were still young and in training. However, the need to maintain Egypt's role as the leader of the Arab Middle East was too large, and Nasser chose risky confrontation to preserve his

---

[94] Elbendary, "The Long Revolution."

reputation rather than pragmatic diplomacy, causing him to rally neighboring Arab states under Egypt's military umbrella. Riding on the confidence gained by his victory in the Suez Crisis, Nasser went to war, believing that rushing in headfirst, with other major Arab states behind him, would cause Israel to rethink its position.

Adding to Nasser's confidence was his strong ties with the other Arab countries, most notably Syria and Jordan. Prior to this, the Egyptian government had worked with the governments of Syria and Jordan to sign a treaty and amass a coordinated military force to defend the Arab countries in the event of an Israeli attack. Nasser likely genuinely believed that should he go to war, the Israeli forces would be no match for the Egyptian-led force armed with quality arms and military equipment supplied by the Soviet Union.[95] Unfortunately for Nasser, he was proved wrong.

On June 5, 1967, Israeli attacks on Egyptian forces began. The undefended Egyptian air force was wiped out on the ground after a strategically targeted surprise air raid by Israeli forces. The attacks caught the Egyptian forces completely off guard, and Nasser was baffled by why his air force had been undefended and so easily wiped out. He demanded an answer from his commander-in-chief, Field Marshal Amer, who only gave vague answers. Amer then abruptly ordered a full withdrawal of Egyptian troops – an order Nasser's friend and Egypt's vice president Anwar Sadat branded as effectively "an order to commit suicide."[96] A bewildered Nasser demanded to know why Amer did not attempt to establish a defense line in the Sinai and ordered an unplanned full withdrawal instead. Amer simply replied that the line – which was to be ready at all times – had not been ready.[97]

In the days that followed, Israeli troops were easily able to march across the Sinai Peninsula, meeting little resistance from the Egyptians, who were no longer able to mount an effective ground offensive deprived of all air cover. By June 9, most of the towns and cities of the Sinai had been seized by Israeli forces, and on June 10, Israel captured the Golan Heights. A ceasefire was signed on June 11, formally marking the defeat of the Arab collation. As the humiliation of the defeat sunk in, Nasser knew the only option was abdication. However, upon announcing his decision to step down, the Egyptian people called for his continued leadership; as such, Nasser stayed on as president. Field Marshal Amer was promptly placed under house arrest for his ineptitude as commander-in-chief, but later committed suicide before any trial could be conducted.[98]

Raw hatred for Israel is a common feature among Arab leaders, and one that Nasser himself could not escape. The Suez crisis had emboldened him greatly, for the taste of victory he experienced then was a large, if not the largest, factor in his decision to begin mobilizing

---

[95] Charles D. Smith, Palestine and the Arab-Israeli Conflict (New York: Bedford/St. Martin's, 2004), 272-273.
[96] George Sullivan, *Sadat: The Man Who Changed Mid-East History* (New York: Walker, 1981), 53.
[97] Carroll, *Anwar Sadat,* 52.
[98] Ibid., 55.

Egyptian troops into the Sinai – this despite the fact that the victory over the canal belonged to the U.S., which had orchestrated the withdrawal of foreign forces from the Canal Zone. Nonetheless, Nasser and much of Egypt had conveniently yet genuinely believed that it was Egypt that had won that crisis. Furthermore, the lack of organization and the sheer number of missteps that the Egyptian army, the leadership, and Nasser himself took during those ill-fated six days were an indication that Egypt and its allies were not even close to being fully prepared for a full-fledged war.

As the most powerful nation in the Arab world and military leader of the Middle East, Egypt had been tasked with leading the Arab defense. Defeat in a war that had only lasted six days was a devastation to the reputation and image of Egypt. But more than this, the humiliation that Nasser felt was severe; his pride was dealt a crippling blow, from which he would never fully recover. He changed physically as well; Anwar Sadat would later write in his autobiography that "Nasser's appearance changed drastically. His eyes turned dull. His smile no longer dazzled. His face and hands took on a sickly pallor. Death seemed to be stalking him."[99]

During the three years following the 1967 war, Nasser progressively lost the confidence of the population of Egypt, as well as that of other Arab states. The loss in the war was a blow not only to Nasser and his ego, but also to his idea of pan-Arabism and the strength of Arab unity. The defeat had showed that even when uniting all of their military forces and resources, the Arab countries were unable to resist Israeli expansion into Arab lands, and even lost key areas. The final blow to the Egyptian people, and proof that Nasser was no longer the man he started out as, was when Egypt signed the Rogers Plan in 1969 – a treaty drafted by the U.S. offering a diplomatic settlement to the 1967 war.[100] To much of the Arab population, the treaty was seen as an accommodation to Western powers and an utter refutation of the pan-Arabism ideology, and Nasser's easy acceptance of it was the final nail in the coffin.

The state of the post-war Egyptian economy was also a great problem. Though the war lasted a mere six days, the amount of resources and funds spent to prepare for it took a large financial toll. Moreover, the loss of the Suez Canal and the oil-rich Sinai Peninsula also equated to a massive loss in revenue for the government. Much of the remaining government funds were diverted from the social projects that had become such a cornerstone of Nasser's popular policies to the rebuilding of the Egyptian military and financial support for the Egyptians displaced from their homes as a result of the war. To make matters worse, the industrial sector that Nasser had spent much time and effort into developing began to stall, and by 1970, the Egyptian economy was on the brink of collapse, no longer able to rely solely on internal sources of revenue to sustain itself. [101]

---

[99] Ibid., 54.

[100] Joseph P. Lorenz, *Egypt and the Arabs: foreign policy and the search for national identity* (Colorado: Westview Press, 1990), 34.

[101] Danielson, "Nasser and Pan-Arabism: Explaining Egypt's Rise in Power," 44.

The 1967 defeat thus caused the Egyptian population and much of the Arab world to question the costs and benefits of a pan-Arabist future. Egyptians preferred to retain their position as leaders of a united Arab entity, but they also realized that they did not want this at the expense of Egyptian territory and pride. Nasser lost much of his political capital, and his popularity began to fade, which led to the weakening of popular support for the government. Though the people demonstrated against his abdication immediately after the 1967 defeat, causing him to withdraw his resignation, they were no longer as confident in the leadership Nasser promised. The population now wanted a say in the future of their country, as shown in the mass demonstration of 1968.[102] In response, Nasser announced his creation of what he called the 30 March Manifesto, which called for the drafting of a new constitution that would reform the Arab Socialist Union (ASU), which was the ruling party that had been formed by Nasser. Sadat later called the manifesto "the last comprehensive program given by Nasser to his nation…critical to the country's desperate need for national unity."[103] However, it was too little too late. Demonstrations continued, this time calling for Nasser's resignation, and from 1968 to 1970, Nasser's popular support plummeted. There was a strong push by the Egyptian population for radical reforms in the government, and Nasser struggled to deliver.

---

[102] Raymond A. Hinnebusch Jr., *Egyptian politics under Sadat: The post-populist development of an authoritarian-modernizing state* (New York: Cambridge University Press, 1985), 37.

[103] Laurie Brand, *Official Stories: Politics and National Narratives in Egypt and Algeria* (Stanford: Stanford University Press, 2014), 70.

Protestors protest against Nasser's resignation in 1967

Nasser and Sadat voting on the 1968 referendum for a new constitution

Nasser and Muammar Gaddafi (right) in Tripoli, Libya in 1969

Chapter 11: Nasser's Death and Legacy

On September 28, 1970, Gamal Abdel Nasser died at his residence in Cairo of a heart attack. Nasser was a heavy smoker with a family history of heart disease – two of his brothers had died in their fifties from the same heart condition.[104] Following the announcement of Nasser's death, the Egyptian people and Arab countries were in a state of shock, as was most of the world. His funeral was momentous and emotional; millions of mourners filled the streets of Cairo and cities across Egypt, weeping over the departure of their revolutionary leader and chanting, "There is no God but Allah, and Nasser is God's beloved…Each of us is Nasser."[105] Several were killed in Beirut from the chaos that followed mourning processions, and in Jerusalem, around 75,000 Arabs marched through the Old City chanting, "Nasser will never die."[106] Anwar Sadat, as the vice president, became acting president.

---

[104] Craig Diagle, *The Limits of Detente: The United States, the Soviet Union, and the Arab–Israeli Conflict, 1969–1973* (New Haven: Yale University Press, 2012), 115.
[105] "Nasser's Legacy: Hope and Instability," *Time*. October 12, 1970, http://content.time.com/time/magazine/article/0,9171,942325-1,00.html.
[106] Ibid.

A picture of Nasser, Yasser Arafat (left), and King Hussein of Jordan taken the day before Nasser's death

A picture of Nasser's funeral procession

Historian Keith Wheelock analyzed the state of Egypt aptly: "Modern Egypt always has been a difficult country to govern. Physical control has been a relatively simple task, for the Egyptians are by nature a submissive people. But positive plans for development continually have been defeated by Egyptian inertia and lack of public responsibility. True, in the past, "strong men" – such as Mohamed Ali, dictator of Egypt for over forty years, and Khedive Ismail – have imposed their will on Egypt. When they passed from the stage, however, their accomplishments were dissipated by the ineptness of their successors and by the apathy of Egypt's ruling classes...few groups were untainted by the corruption which permeated Cairo."[107]

Thus, the task Nasser faced as leader of the newly formed Egyptian Republic was one that was immense as well as doomed. His aggressive plunge into risky wars and conflicts were not done out of sheer hubris or crazed pride; he knew that it took great power and bold actions for Egypt to regain its former glory.

Throughout the history of the Middle East, there has always been a widespread contention that Arab countries in the region have not been able to unite or find commonalities among their various policies, cultures, and causes. However, this contention should be discarded, as it is quite clear that starting from the early twentieth century, pan-Arabism as an ideology and political strategy increasingly had great impact on regional politics. In fact, Gamal Abdel Nasser's presidency was a key accelerant in the spreading of pan-Arabism, as Nasser himself espoused the idea and utilized it to profoundly increase Egypt's importance in the Middle East and vault its influence on the world stage. With this increased power, Nasser worked on social, political, and economic policies to make Egypt strong domestically, while in the foreign arena, he focused on non-alignment and military neutrality when maneuvering through the fickle and volatile politics of the Cold War, thereby increasing Egypt's prominence as leader of the Non-Alignment Movement and boosting its influence further.

In order to bring about this success on the world stage, Nasser worked hard to strengthen his country domestically, implementing key social and economic policies designed to unite the country behind his leadership. As can be seen throughout history, when it comes to the rise and fall of nations, strong leadership is not the only essential factor – a country united behind such a leader is also key. Nasser was no exception; he pursued policies and enacted laws that guaranteed his sole ascendancy to power, including the comprehensive banning of social and political groups that did not support his government, radical changes in the agricultural sector that overhauled the socioeconomic class structures of Egyptian society, and so on.

This was likely the cornerstone of Nasser's legacy – the immense focus he placed on unity, consolidation of power, and pan-Arabism. His political strategies all ultimately centered on this idea. An apt example of this is his utilization of the Muslim Brotherhood pre-revolution, then comparing this with his policies toward the group post-revolution. The Muslim Brotherhood and

---

[107] Wheelock, *Nasser's New Egypt,* 277.

Nasser's Free Officers had shared a common goal before and during the revolution – Egyptian liberation from the shackles of British imperialism and the overhaul of the entire government. Thus, the relationship between the two sides had been that of cooperation, tolerance, and support. However, once the revolution was achieved and Nasser gained power, Nasser realized that there were grave and possibly dangerous differences in his goals and those of the Muslim Brotherhood – the main one being that the Brotherhood sought the establishment of an Islamic state based on *shari'a* laws, whereas Nasser was working to build a modern and largely secular state. Nasser began oppressing the Muslim Brotherhood, rounding up its leaders and sending troops to stop its demonstrations, and the oppression became more severe after he experienced an attempted assassination orchestrated by a Brotherhood member. For the rest of Nasser's presidency, Muslim Brotherhood members were arrested, tortured, harassed, and exiled.[108] Nasser's way of rule was black or white – he allowed no opposition or challenge to his rule.

Nonetheless, Nasser's legacy is also that of the immense popularity he was able to garner from his people. Nasser focused on positive reforms and nationwide social services in return for the people's political support. Under this social contract, the Egyptian government began providing health care services, food subsidies, improved and more widespread education, rent control, and low-cost housing. For example, health care was a dire problem in Egypt during the British occupation; the system developed by the British did not allow most citizens access to quality health care, as many could not afford it. Nasser vowed to provide, at the very least, basic health care services to all Egyptian citizens, and to accomplish this, he drastically increased funding to the health care system and the Ministry of Public Health, leading to a surge in the number of registered doctors from 4470 in 1952 to 6420 in 1956.[109] Similar reforms were made in the education sector; under Nasser's direction, between 1955 and 1964, approximately 4,000 primary schools were constructed throughout Egypt, available for all children to attend.[110] This social contract was received with enthusiasm by the Egyptian people. For the first time in decades, a strong Egyptian ruler had emerged who could actually provide for the needs of the people and was deserving of their support.

While strengthening the country domestically, Nasser never forgot his goal of pan-Arabism and intra-Arab political cooperation; he always understood that there was an important connection between Egypt's domestic and foreign policies, stating at one cabinet meeting that "our foreign policy is in service to our internal policy."[111] This and many other ideas he had for the future of Egypt and the Middle East were broadcasted regionally on the transnational Egyptian radio program, *Voice of the Arabs,* which was established by Nasser himself in 1954 to ensure that he had a direct outlet to the entire Arab population.[112] He also worked to increase the

---

[108] Bjorn Olav Utvik, "Filling the vacant throne of Nasser: The economic discourse of Egypt's Islamist Opposition," *Arab Studies Quarterly* 17, no. 4 (Fall 1995), 31.
[109] Wheelock, *Nasser's New Egypt: A Critical Analysis*, 132.
[110] Ibid., 112.
[111] Yahya, *Egypt and the Soviet Union, 1952-1972: A study in the power of the small state,* 142.
[112] Jankowski, *Nasser's Egypt, Arab Nationalism, and the United Arab Republic,* 55.

circulation of Egyptian media and newspapers to other Arab countries, particularly neighboring Jordan, Lebanon, and Syria. All these efforts to have his voice heard in other Arab countries and unify them were again part of his dreams of uniting the entire Arab population, in line with the concept of pan-Arabism.

Gamal Abdel Nasser was a strong leader, willing to go out on a limb for what he believed in. His propensity to charge forward and take risks allowed him to further his vision for his country and bolster Egypt's role in the region; however, it was also what marked his end, as he rushed into a war without assessing the costs and benefits, blinded by his pride and his large dreams. Though his fall was not as quick and dramatic as his rise, his death brought grief across the Middle East in a way no other Arab leader had. Gamal Abdel Nasser thus left a decidedly significant mark on the history and politics of both Egypt and the Middle East.

Bibliography

Abdel Nasser, Hoda. "A Historical Sketch of Gamal Abdel Nasser." *Bibliotheca Alexandria*. http://nasser.bibalex.org/Common/pictures01-%20sira_en.htm#1.

Aburish, Said K. *Nasser: The Last Arab* (New York: St. Martin's Press, 2004).

Alexander, Anne. *Nasser Life and Times* (London: Haus Publishing, 2005).

Benin, Joel. *The Dispersion of Egyptian Jewry: Culture, Politics, and the Formation of a Modern Diaspora*. Cairo: American University in Cairo Press, 2005.

Brand, Laurie. *Official Stories: Politics and National Narratives in Egypt and Algeria*. Stanford: Stanford University Press, 2014.

Brightman, Carol. *Total Insecurity: The Myth of American Omnipotence*. London: Verso, 2004.

Butt, Gerald. "Lesson From History: 1955 Baghdad Pact." *BBC News*. February 26, 2003. http://news.bbc.co.uk/2/hi/middle_east/2801487.stm.

Carroll, Raymond. *Anwar Sadat*. New York: F. Watts, 1982.

Coury, Ralph M. "Who "Invented Egyptian Arab Nationalism? Part 2." *International Journal of Middle East Studies* 14, no. 4 (November 1982): 459-479.

Danielson, Robert Eugene "Nasser and Pan-Arabism: Explaining Egypt's Rise in Power." MA diss., Naval Postgraduate School, 2007.

Dawisha, Adeed. *Arab Nationalism in the Twentieth Century: From Triumph to Despair*. Princeton: Princeton University Press, 2003.

Diagle, Craig. *The Limits of Detente: The United States, the Soviet Union, and the Arab–Israeli Conflict, 1969–1973.* New Haven: Yale University Press, 2012.

El-Sadat, Anwar. *Those I Have Known.* New York: Continuum, 1984.

Elbendary, Amina. "The Long Revolution." *Al-Ahram.* July 18, 2002. http://weekly.ahram.org.eg/2002/595/sc2.htm.

Finklestone, Joseph *Anwar Sadat: Visionary Who Dared.* London: Frank Cass Publishers, 1996.

Gershoni, Israel. *The Emergence of Pan-Arabism in Egypt.* Israel: Tel Aviv University, 1981.

Gordon, Joel. *Nasser: Hero of the Arab Nation.* Oxford: Oneworld Publications, 2006.

Gordon, Joel. *Nasser's Blessed Movement: Egypt's Free Officers and the July Revolution.* New York: Oxford University Press, 1992.

Hamad, Mahmoud "When the Gavel Speaks: Judicial Politics in Modern Egypt." PhD diss., University of Utah, 2008.

Haykal, Muhammad Hasanayn *The Cairo Documents: The Inside Story of Nasser and His Relationship with World Leaders, Rebels, and Statesmen.* New York: Doubleday, 1973.

Hinnebusch, Raymond A. *Egyptian Politics under Sadat: The Post-Populist Development of an Authoritarian-Modernizing State.* New York: Cambridge University Press, 1985.

Jankowski, James. *Arab Nationalism in "Nasserism" and Egyptian State Policy, 1952-1958 in Rethinking Nationalism in the Arab Middle East,* edited by James Jankowski and Israel Gershoni. New York: Columbia University Press, 1997.

Jankowski, James. *Nasser's Egypt, Arab Nationalism, and the United Arab Republic.* Colorado: Lynne Rienner Publishers, 2002.

Khalidi, Rashid. "Arab Nationalism: Historical Problems in the Literature," *The American Historical Review* 96, no. 5 (December 1991): 1363-1373.

Khalidi, Rashid. *The Origins of Arab Nationalism: Introduction in The Origins of Arab Nationalism,* edited by Rashid Khalidi, Lisa Anderson, Muhammad Muslih, and Reeva S. Simon. New York: Columbia University Press, 1991.

Lacouture, Jean. *The Demigods: Charismatic Leadership in the Third World.* New York: Knopf, 1970.

Lewis, Bernard. *The Multiple Identities of the Middle East.* New York: Schocken Books, 1998.

Lorenz, Joseph P. *Egypt and the Arabs: Foreign Policy and the Search for National Identity.* Colorado: Westview Press, 1990.

Metz, Helen Chapin. Ed. *Egypt: A Country Study.* Washington: GPO for the Library of Congress, 1990.

"Nasser's Legacy: Hope and Instability." *Time.* October 12, 1970. http://content.time.com/time/magazine/article/0,9171,942325-1,00.html.

Osman, Tarek. *Egypt on the Brink.* New Haven: Yale University Press, 2010.

Podeh, Elie and Onn Winckler. "Introduction: Nasserism as a Form of Populism." In *Rethinking Nasserism: Revolution and Historical Memory in Modern* Egypt, edited by Elie Podeh and Onn Winckler, 10-42. Gainesville, FL: University Press of Florida, 2004.

Smith, Charles D. *Palestine and the Arab-Israeli Conflict.* New York: Bedford/St. Martin's, 2004).

Sullivan, George. *Sadat: The Man Who Changed Mid-East History.* New York: Walker, 1981.

Tristam, Pierre. "Gamal Abdel Nasser: Profile (1918-1970)." http://middleeast.about.com/od/egypt/p/Gamal-Abdel-Nasser-Profile.htm.

"United Arab Republic." http://countrystudies.us/syria/14.htm.

Utvik, Bjorn Olav. "Filling the Vacant Throne of Nasser: The Economic Discourse of Egypt's Islamist Opposition." *Arab Studies Quarterly* 17, no. 4 (Fall 1995): 25-94.

Warburg, Gabriel. "Lampson's Ultimatum to Faruq, 4 February, 1942." *Middle Eastern Studies* 11, no. 1 (1975): 24-32.

Wheelock, Keith. *Nasser's New Egypt.* New York: Frederick A. Prager, Inc., 1960.

Witte, Sam. *Gamal Abdel Nasser* (New York: Rosen, 2004.

Yahya, Ali M. *Egypt and the Soviet Union, 1952-1972: A Study in the Power of the Small State.* PhD diss., University Microfilms International, Indiana University, 1981.

Printed in Great Britain
by Amazon.co.uk, Ltd.,
Marston Gate.